CONTENTS

Christian Basics Bible Studies

Knowing Christ is where faith begins. From there we grow through the essentials of discipleship: Bible study, prayer, Christian community and much more. We learn to set godly priorities, grow in Christian character and witness to others. We persevere through doubts and grow in wisdom. These are the topics woven into each of the Christian Basics Bible Studies. Working through this series will help you become a more mature Christian.

WHAT KIND OF GUIDE IS THIS?

The studies are not designed to merely tell you what one person thinks. Instead, through inductive study, they will help you discover for yourself what Scripture is saying. Each study deals with a particular passage—rather than jumping around the Bible—so that you can really delve into the author's meaning in that context.

The studies ask three different kinds of questions. *Observation* questions help you to understand the content of the passage by asking about the basic facts: who, what, when, where and how. *Interpretation* questions delve into the meaning of the passage. *Application* questions help you discover its implications for growing in Christ.

These three keys unlock the treasures of the biblical writings and help you live them out.

This is a thought-provoking guide. Each question assumes a variety of answers. Many questions do not have "right" answers, particularly questions that aim at meaning or application. Instead, the questions should inspire users to explore the passage more thoroughly.

This study guide is flexible. You can use it for individual study, but it is also great for a variety of groups—student, professional, neighborhood or church groups. Each study takes about forty-five minutes in a group setting or thirty minutes in personal study.

How They're Put Together

Each study is composed of four sections: opening paragraphs and questions to help you get into the topic, the NIV text and questions that invite study of the passage, questions to help you apply what you have learned, and a suggestion for prayer.

The workbook format provides space for writing a response to each question. This format is ideal for personal study and allows group members to prepare in advance for the discussion and/or write down notes during the study. This space can form a permanent record of your thoughts and spiritual progress.

At the back of the guide are study notes that may be useful for leaders or for individuals. These notes do not give "the answers," but they do provide additional background information on certain questions to help you through the difficult spots. The "Guidelines for Leaders" section describes how to lead a group discussion, gives helpful tips on group dynamics and suggests ways to deal with problems that may arise during the discussion. With such helps, someone with little or no experience can lead an effective group study.

SUGGESTIONS FOR INDIVIDUAL STUDY

1. This guide is based on a classic book or booklet that will enrich your spiritual life. If you have not read the book or booklet suggested in the "Further Reading" section, you may want to read the portion suggested before you begin your study. The ideas in the book will enhance your study, but the Bible text will be the focus of each session.

2. Read the introduction. Consider the opening questions and note your responses.

3. Pray, asking God to speak to you from his Word about this particular topic.

4. Read the passage reproduced for you from the New International Version. You may wish to mark phrases that seem important. Note in the margin any questions that come to your mind as you read.

5. Use the questions from the study guide to more thoroughly examine the passage. Note your findings in the space provided. After you have made your own notes, read the corresponding study notes in the back of the book for further insights.

6. Reread the entire passage, making further notes about its general principles and about the way you intend to use them.

7. Move to the "Commit" section. Spend time prayerfully considering what the passage has to say specifically to your life.

8. Read the suggestion for prayer. Speak to God about insights you have gained. Tell him of any desires you have for specific growth. Ask him to help you as you attempt to live out the principles described in that passage.

Suggestions for Members of a Group Study

Joining a Bible study group can be a great avenue to spiritual growth. Here are a few guidelines that will help you as you participate in the studies in this guide.

1. Reading the book suggested as further reading, before or after each session, will enhance your study and understanding of the themes in this guide.

2. These studies focus on a particular passage of Scripture—in depth. Only rarely should you refer to other portions of the Bible, and then only at the request of the leader. Of course, the Bible is internally consistent. Other good forms of study draw on that consistency, but inductive Bible study sticks with a single passage and works on it in depth.

3. These are discussion studies. Questions in this guide aim at helping a group discuss together a passage of Scripture in order to understand its content, meaning and implications. Most people are either natural talkers or natural listeners, yet this type of study works best if people participate more or less evenly. Try to curb any natural tendency to either excessive talking or excessive quiet. You and the rest of the group will benefit.

4. Most questions in this guide allow for a variety of answers. If you disagree with someone else's comment, gently say so. Then explain your own point of view from the passage before you.

5. Be willing to lead a discussion, if asked. Much of the preparation for leading has already been accomplished in the writing of this guide.

6. Respect the privacy of people in your group. Many people speak

of things within the context of a Bible study/prayer group that they do not want to be public knowledge. Assume that personal information spoken within the group setting is private, unless you are specifically told otherwise. And don't talk about it elsewhere.

7. We recommend that all groups follow a few basic guidelines and that these guidelines be read at the first session. The guidelines, which you may wish to adapt to your situation, are the following:

   a. Anything said in this group is considered confidential and will not be discussed outside the group unless specific permission is given to do so.

   b. We will provide time for each person present to talk if he or she feels comfortable doing so.

   c. We will talk about ourselves and our own situations, avoiding conversation about other people.

   d. We will listen attentively to each other.

   e. We will pray for each other.

8. Enjoy your study. Prepare to grow.

SUGGESTIONS FOR GROUP LEADERS

There are specific suggestions to help you in leading in the "Guidelines for Leaders" and in the "Study Notes" at the back of this guide. Read the "Guidelines for Leaders" carefully, even if you are only leading one group meeting. Then you can go to the section on the particular session you will lead.

The Wisdom of Proverbs

Who would have guessed that a series of books ". . . for Dummies" would sell more than thirty-five million copies? These self-education books have been purchased by people like you and me who wish they knew more than they do about a particular subject. With more than one hundred separate titles, the series offers expert advice for just about everyone.

Why has this series so effectively tapped into the desire of people to learn? One satisfied customer said: "I buy them because they take the intimidation out of the learning process. Whatever the subject matter, they spell it out to me in simple terms. They make the complex understandable, so that even a regular guy like me can 'get it.' "

The same could be said for the book of Proverbs. It takes the ageless, priceless wisdom of God himself and makes it understandable and accessible to regular people like you and me. The most down-to-earth book in the Bible, Proverbs puts pertinent truths for everyday life on the bottom shelf where we can all reach them.

THE BOOK OF PROVERBS

The unity of the message of Proverbs is remarkable, considering that most biblical scholars believe that it is a collection of sayings written by a number of different wise people. The collection was compiled primarily during the period of Israel's history when it was ruled by kings, several hundred years before the birth of Christ. In fact, many of the more than five hundred proverbs are attributed to King Solomon, who has been called the wisest man who ever lived.

Proverbs was not written as a book of promises or rigid rules about life. As it says in the introduction to the book in *The Student Bible*:

> Anybody with a brain can find exceptions to Proverbs' generalities. For example, Proverbs 28:19 proclaims that "he who works his land will have abundant food, but the one who chases fantasies will have his fill of poverty." Yet farmers who work hard go hungry in a drought, and dreamers win $10 million in a lottery. *Proverbs simply tells how life works most of the time.* You can worry about the exceptions after you have learned the rule. (p. 561, italics added)

The Proverbs are written in the poetic forms of the Hebrew culture of that day. Many of them are written in couplets (a pair of successive lines of verse) that make a statement and then repeat it in a slightly different form.

Sometimes the writer drives home his point by setting up contrasts. Some proverbs paint graphic word pictures with rich and colorful language. On the other hand, some proverbs are so plain and simple, we almost pass them by—but we shouldn't. The book of Proverbs also has a sense of humor; and despite its poetic elegance, the book rarely minces words.

Above all, Proverbs is about wisdom—the heavenly wisdom of God that he graciously shares with us so we can live wisely here on earth.

It's About Wisdom

What is wisdom? Wisdom is what is true and right combined with good judgment. Other words that fit under the umbrella of the biblical concept of wisdom are *discerning, judicious, prudent* and *sensible*.

Not very glamorous words, perhaps, but words you can build a life on.

One of the incomparable benefits of pursuing wisdom is that it offers us a navigational system to keep us out of moral blind alleys and dead-end roads. "Discretion will protect you, and understanding will guard you. Wisdom will save you from the ways of wicked men, from men whose words are perverse, who leave the straight paths to walk in dark ways" (Proverbs 2:11-13).

Pursuing wisdom is also an effective way of investing in the future. "If you find it, there is a future hope for you, and your hope will not be cut off" (Proverbs 24:14). What kind of hope does wisdom offer us for the future? Undoubtedly hope for a future in heaven but also, I believe, hope for a life that works . . . here, today, in this world.

The wisdom of Proverbs can make our lives work better. These studies will show you how.

For further reading: Each study is drawn from themes in one or two of the chapters of *Making Life Work.* You'll find suggested reading at the end of each study. Since only six sessions are in this guide, and the topics are diverse, you will not find every chapter covered here.

Pursue Wisdom

Proverbs 2:1-15

Time and again I have seen the positive impact of pursuing wisdom. I can think of a number of people I know who have neither dazzling talents, stellar credentials nor charismatic personalities but who nonetheless have risen to places of strategic importance in the marketplace, in government, in academia, in the nonprofit sector and in the church. These people have gained responsibility and respect for one reason: they have handled themselves wisely in their workplace over a long time. In their work and their relationships on the job, they have applied wisdom from the book of Proverbs—wisdom about taking initiative and developing discipline, wisdom about speaking the truth in love and managing anger and doing good to others. The foolish people around them who neglected these principles eventually fell by the wayside, but these wise people are still on the job—and still receiving honor and reward.

OPEN

■ Who are some wise people you have known, and how did you know they were wise?

■ What are some results of foolishness?

■ Think of decisions you have made which you believe were wise. What moved you to act with wisdom in those situations?

 ## STUDY

Read Proverbs 2:1-15.

¹My son, if you accept my words
    and store up my commands within you,
²turning your ear to wisdom
    and applying your heart to understanding,
³and if you call out for insight
    and cry aloud for understanding,
⁴and if you look for it as for silver
    and search for it as for hidden treasure,
⁵then you will understand the fear of the LORD
    and find the knowledge of God.
⁶For the LORD gives wisdom,
    and from his mouth come knowledge and understanding.
⁷He holds victory in store for the upright,
    he is a shield to those whose walk is blameless.
⁸for he guards the course of the just
    and protects the way of his faithful ones.

⁹Then you will understand what is right and just
    and fair—every good path.
¹⁰For wisdom will enter your heart,
    and knowledge will be pleasant to your soul.
¹¹Discretion will protect you,
    and understanding will guard you.

¹²Wisdom will save you from the ways of wicked men,
    from men whose words are perverse,
¹³who leave the straight paths
    to walk in dark ways,
¹⁴who delight in doing wrong
    and rejoice in the perverseness of evil,
¹⁵whose paths are crooked
    and who are devious in their ways.

---

1. What are the responsibilities of the person who wants to become wise (vv. 1-4)?

---

2. Why are "silver" and "hidden treasure" good metaphors for wisdom (v. 4)?

3. Consider the verbs in verses 3-4. Besides wisdom, what are some other things for which people "call out," "cry aloud," "look" and "search"?

_____

4. Why is wisdom superior to these alternate pursuits?

_____

5. What do you think it means to "understand the fear of the LORD" (v. 5)?

_____

6. According to verse 6, the Lord is the giver of wisdom, knowledge and understanding. If these qualities are gifts from God, why do we need to seek them so diligently?

_____

7. When have you been moved to cry out for wisdom from God?

How did God answer you?

---

8. This passage promises protection (vv. 7, 8, 11, 12-15). What dangers will wisdom protect us from?

---

9. Give some examples of what these dangers would look like in our context.

---

10. When have you been rescued from spiritual or physical danger by wisdom—your own or someone else's?

COMMIT

- Identify an area in which you have not sought God's wisdom. It may be an area in which you have charged ahead and not waited for God. Or it may be an area in which you have lagged back, sought God's wisdom only halfheartedly and not gone ahead as you should. Prayerfully open this area of your life to God's ideas about what is best.

Cry out to God for wisdom, and stay open to accepting his answers. Thank God for the treasure of his wisdom.

For further reading: *Chapter one of* Making Life Work.

Develop Discipline
Proverbs 6:6-11, 20-24

When it comes to the work of living, Proverbs tells us that the most indispensable tool available to all of us is *discipline*. Without it we cannot live productive, satisfying lives. Proverbs 13:18 says, "He who ignores discipline comes to poverty and shame." While poverty and shame may manifest themselves in many forms, ignoring discipline always manifests itself in a life sliding toward ruin. If we fail to take discipline seriously, we do so at our own peril.

The notion of discipline often conjures up negative images framed in punitive terms: we envision a child being spanked, a soldier being yelled at or a student being expelled. Or we think of discipline as an unavoidable evil, as an oppressive pattern of rigid routines and daily deprivations, imposed on us by some outside force determined to make our lives miserable. According to this view, discipline is the enemy, the obvious foe of a happy, meaningful life.

But not everyone views discipline that way. I recently read an article about a woman who wins many of the Chicago marathons in the wheelchair division. When she was asked how she manages to do well so consistently, she said that she disciplines herself to train in her wheelchair one hundred miles each week. She sees this form of discipline as the only means of maintaining her competitive edge. It is the tool she uses to develop the strength and speed and endurance she wants to have.

If we dream of fulfilling our highest potential educationally and vocationally, we need discipline. If we dream of being a spouse, a parent or a friend who breathes life into other people, if we dream of honoring God with our finances and serving others with our money, if we dream of using our spiritual gifts in meaningful ways, if we dream of maintaining physical health through diet and exercise, we need discipline.

 OPEN

- Would you say you are basically lazy or hard-working? Why do you have that opinion?

- Where do you find it hard to be disciplined?

- Where do you find it easiest to be disciplined?

 STUDY

Read Proverbs 6:6-11, 20-24.

⁶Go to the ant, you sluggard;

consider its ways and be wise!
[7]It has no commander,
no overseer or ruler,
[8]yet it stores its provisions in summer
and gathers its food at harvest.

[9]How long will you lie there, you sluggard?
When will you get up from your sleep?
[10]A little sleep, a little slumber,
a little folding of the hands to rest—
[11]and poverty will come on you like a bandit
and scarcity like an armed man.

[20]My son, keep your father's commands
and do not forsake your mother's teaching.
[21]Bind them upon your heart forever;
fasten them around your neck.
[22]When you walk, they will guide you;
when you sleep, they will watch over you;
when you awake, they will speak to you.
[23]For these commands are a lamp,
this teaching a light,
and the corrections of discipline
are the way to life,
[24]keeping you from the immoral woman,
from the smooth tongue of the wayward wife.

---

1. What is remarkable about what the ant can accomplish (vv. 6-8)?

2. How is the ant rewarded for its hard work?

_____

3. To human observation, the ant appears to work non-stop. No doubt it has periods of inactivity, underground and out of sight. If the writer of Proverbs is not telling us to work twenty-four hours a day, what is he saying we should learn from the ant?

_____

4. What are some results of laziness (such as pictured in v. 9)?

_____

5. It seems unlikely that "a little" sleep or rest would cause someone to come to ruin (vv. 10-11). Why is this "little" so dangerous?

_____

6. What are some practical ways to discipline ourselves to obey the instructions of verses 20-21?

7. Verse 22 names three situations in which wisdom will protect us. The three situations—walking, sleeping and waking—actually cover all of life. How has wisdom guided you or helped you in one of these situations?

___ someone or something stopped you from acting on a temptation

___ a friend told you about something that God has done in his or her own life that gave you courage to face a hard time

___ a dream helped you in seeking God's direction

___ a verse of Scripture came to your mind just as you awakened, and you found that it was exactly what you needed that day

___ other _____

_____

8. Verse 24 promises that God's commands will protect the obedient person from sexual sin. Why does this type of sin particularly require discipline if we are going to avoid it?

_____

9. The "commands" and "corrections of discipline" of verse 23 are ultimately God's commands and discipline. They are described as a light and the way to life. Why is a well-lighted path such a good description of consistent obedience to God?

10. What image or idea from this study would you like to draw on for
    encouragement?

 COMMIT

- Reflect on where you have slacked off in your responsibilities to
  the Lord, to others, and to your own spiritual and physical health.
  Decide how you need and want to change, and make specific
  plans to apply discipline in each of those areas of life.

Ask God to renew your discipline and help you keep your commitments.

For further reading: *Chapter four of* Making Life Work.

Speak Truth

Proverbs 11:1, 3; 12:19, 22; 14:25; 15:4

Do you remember the first time you were betrayed or lied to? The first time a confidence was broken or the truth twisted in order to hurt you?

Lying is always going to be a messy business because we're created in the image of a truth-telling God. At the core of the character of God is an essence of purity that renders him incapable of dishonesty. Because of the piece of that purity that is at our own core, it will always feel unnatural and incongruous for us to lie. There will always be warning bells and whistles going off in our minds and that sick feeling in our stomachs. We weren't created to lie.

But there's another side to truth telling. When a given situation demands that a word of truth be spoken, we are commanded to speak it without hesitating, without holding back and without considering the cost to ourselves, even if it costs us dearly.

The ugly truth about me is that too often I choose peacekeeping over truth telling. I silence words of truth because they might create ripples on the pond of my life, and I, like many people, am a tranquility junkie. I want smooth waters, not rough seas.

We can't control anyone else's choice to speak truth or to tell lies. But we can make that choice for ourselves. We can take the necessary steps to become loving truth-tellers.

OPEN

- As you read the introduction, how would you rate your level of comfort?

  ___ I feel totally relaxed about this issue.

  ___ I'm a little uncomfortable.

  ___ I feel very nervous.

  ___ I didn't want to read it.

  ___ I'd rather not even think about honesty.

- Would you say you tend to prefer peacekeeping or truth telling?

- When have you especially appreciated someone's honesty?

 STUDY

Read Proverbs 11:1, 3.

[1]The LORD abhors dishonest scales,
    but accurate weights are his delight.

[3]The integrity of the upright guides them,
    but the unfaithful are destroyed by their duplicity.

1. The image of verse 1 is a marketplace where a merchant weighs out goods. Consider the fact that God delights in the fairness of a purchase of a few pounds of wheat or meat. What does that tell you about God's concern for the everyday dealings of our lives?

2. Integrity is a quality that can bring us admiration. How can it also guide us (v. 3)?

3. *Duplicity* (v. 3) is also translated *dishonesty, falseness, perversity* and *crookedness.* People often feel they can get ahead through dishonesty—in fact some people think it's the only way to get ahead. How can dishonesty eventually destroy a person?

Read Proverbs 12:19, 22.

[19]Truthful lips endure forever,
    but a lying tongue lasts only a moment.

[22]The LORD detests lying lips,
    but he delights in men who are truthful.

4. What comfort does verse 19 offer a person who has been a victim of another's dishonesty?

_____

5. How does verse 19 encourage us to trust God?

_____

6. Verse 22 uses emotional language to describe God's attitude toward lying and toward honesty. How would you describe the contrast?

_____

7. Proverbs 14:25 says, "A truthful witness saves lives, but a false witness is deceitful." In what situations could a truthful witness literally save lives?

_____

8. Proverbs 15:4 says, "The tongue that brings healing is a tree of life, but a deceitful tongue crushes the spirit." How do we know that the healing tongue is also a tongue that tells the truth?

9. In what senses do honest words bring healing and life?

_____

10. Where is it most difficult for you to be honest? Consider both outright lies and timidity about speaking the truth.

COMMIT

■ Confess any dishonesty you've committed toward God and others.

■ Resolve to stop lying. If we have even the slightest tendency to distort the truth—and who among us doesn't?—we need to say, "From this day forward I purpose in my heart, with the help of God, to speak only the truth, always and in every situation, for the rest of my life." Such a commitment will inevitably improve our relationship with God and with everyone else.

Ask the Lord to remove falsehood from you and make you increasingly honest. Thank him that he always tells us the truth.

For further reading: _Chapter five of_ Making Life Work.

Honor Family

Proverbs 15:17; 17:1, 6;
19:18; 21:9, 19; 23:22

The only kind of marriage the writer of Proverbs understands is a lifelong marriage. He would patiently listen to all the current banter about no-fault divorces and serial marriages, and then he would say again, "Rejoice in the spouse of your youth. When you get married, stay married. Make compromises. Get help. Work it out. Fast, pray, try and try and try again. Do whatever you have to do to stay together. Make the most out of your marriage. There is no other way. Strong marriages are the key to strong families." The greater the security between mates, the greater the security children will have in their relationships with their parents, with their siblings, with themselves and with God.

Speaking from the experience of having reared two children to college age, I can say that achieving a delicate balance between love and limits has been one of the greatest challenges of my life. When do we say, "Kids will be kids," and give them some slack, and when do we say, "That behavior or attitude crosses the line. It must be dealt with"? When do we intervene in our children's decision-making processes in order to protect them from hurtful or destructive decisions, and when do we stand back and let our children learn through the hard lessons of life?

Those questions have driven me to my knees time and time again. But I have discovered that it is not a bad place for parents to be. When we come to God with a spirit of humility and seek his wisdom, he offers us his help through Scripture, through books, through mature friends, through counselors and through the personal guidance of the Holy Spirit.

OPEN

■ What are two of the best family memories you can recall?

STUDY

Read Proverbs 15:17; 17:1.

[17]Better a meal of vegetables where there is love
    than a fattened calf with hatred.

[1]Better a dry crust with peace and quiet
    than a house full of feasting, with strife.

1. How would you paraphrase the message of these two verses?

2. Many of the "rich and famous" go through multiple marriages

and spend little time with their own children. Why do you think they remain the objects of so many people's envy?

Read Proverbs 21:9, 19.

⁹Better to live on the corner of the roof
   than share a house with a quarrelsome wife.

¹⁹Better to live in a desert
   than with a quarrelsome and ill-tempered wife.

3. Briefly describe what you think it would be like to live on the corner of a flat rooftop or in a desert (minus an air-conditioned house and an irrigated lawn!).

4. How would the above living situations be better than living with a quarrelsome and ill-tempered spouse?

5. Why is it so easy to be quarrelsome and ill-tempered with the people we are closest to?

6. Proverbs 19:18 says, "Discipline your son, for in that there is hope; do not be a willing party to his death." Recall a time as a child when you were disciplined in a loving way, if not by a parent then by a teacher or other adult. What were the long-term results?

7. How does disciplining children offer them hope?

8. Consider the discipline of God when we do wrong. How does God's discipline offer us hope rather than death?

9. Proverbs 17:6 says, "Children's children are a crown to the aged, and parents are the pride of their children." Describe this proverb's picture of the mutual attitude parents and children should have toward one another.

10. Do you know a family that has this kind of mutual love between

parents and children? What is it like?

---

11. How could you express your appreciation to your parents for what they have done for you?

 COMMIT

■ Consider how you might tend to blame other family members for problems. Search your heart for ways that you might contribute to problems through your actions, words or attitudes. Commit yourself to change with the Lord's help.

■ Resolve to be a godly family member, whether or not you have a godly family.

Thank God for the gift of family. Even if your own family experience has been marred by sin, thank him for the living examples of healthy families you have known. Pray for his blessings of peace and mutual understanding on your family.

For further reading: *Chapters seven, eight and nine of* Making Life Work.

Manage Anger

Proverbs 12:18; 15:1; 16:32;
19:19; 22:24-25; 29:22

In English usage, in the United States at least, we have almost come to use the words *angry* and *mad* interchangeably. It has become common for kids to warn each other by saying, "Watch out. Mom (or Dad) is mad!" Coworkers alert each other to potential risk by saying, "Steer clear. The boss is mad!" Spouses push each other away by saying, "Give me a little space. I'm mad!"

But are the concepts of anger and madness interchangeable? Does anger always have to manifest itself in the kind of frenzied behavior that is destructive, dangerous, out of control, violent and, yes, sinful?

From God's Word, one thing we know about anger is that God created us with the capacity to get angry. Scripture describes God's righteous anger; in passage after passage we read that "God's anger was kindled" against sin, rebellion, evil and injustice. Psalm 30:5 says that God's "anger lasts only a moment, but his favor lasts a lifetime." While the psalmist was confident that God's anger is never the end of the story, he did not deny God's anger. God's anger is real and intense, a force to be dealt with. As creatures made in his image, we have that same capacity to experience strong feelings of anger.

If God himself gets angry, anger is not a bad or sinful emotion that inevitably leads to bad or sinful behavior. Just as God's anger is right-eous, so our anger can energize us to take actions that are good and right and honorable.

Every manifestation of anger requires us to look deep inside at our underlying attitudes. But when it comes to circumstantial anger that is often driven by egoism, preoccupation with our own welfare or an extreme sense of entitlement, a careful examination of our attitudes is essential. Our character growth depends on it.

 ## OPEN

- What makes you really angry?

- Are there things that used to make you angry that you find you can now handle more calmly? What has made the difference?

 ## STUDY

Read Proverbs 19:19; 22:24-25; 29:22.

¹⁹A hot-tempered man must pay the penalty;
> if you rescue him, you will have to do it again.

²⁴Do not make friends with a hot-tempered man,
> do not associate with one easily angered,
²⁵or you may learn his ways
> and get yourself ensnared.

²²An angry man stirs up dissension,
 and a hot-tempered one commits many sins.

---

1. What sort of penalties does a hot-tempered person pay (19:19)?

---

2. When you are angry, how do you respond to people who try to "rescue" you—reason with you, try to get you to calm down or forget about it (19:19)?

---

3. What are some dangers of associating with a hot-tempered person (22:24-25)?

---

4. Suggest some examples of the "many sins" that an angry person may commit (29:22).

5. Do you find it easier to deal with your own anger or other people's anger? Why?

Read Proverbs 12:18; 15:1.
[18]Reckless words pierce like a sword,
   but the tongue of the wise brings healing.

[1]A gentle answer turns away wrath,
   but a harsh word stirs up anger.

_____

6. When have you seen wise words bring healing to yourself or to someone else (12:18)?

_____

7. How do reckless words resemble swords (12:18)?

_____

8. Why is a gentle answer so disarming (15:1)?

9. How does anger snowball into more anger (15:1)?

---

10. Proverbs 16:32 says, "Better a patient man than a warrior, a man who controls his temper than one who takes a city." What strategies have you found for controlling your temper?

COMMIT

■ In what situations do you typically lose control and blow up?

■ Plan a strategy for how you will deal with your anger the next time you want to blow up at someone.

Gentleness and self-control are gifts of the Holy Spirit (Galatians 5:23). As you bring your anger to the Lord, have no fear that he will reject you. God delights in our desire to be self-controlled people.

For further reading: Chapter eleven of Making Life Work.

Trust God

Proverbs 3:1-12

Soon after I became a Christian, I did what most new believers do: I quietly considered how seriously I intended to take my newfound faith. I realized that Jesus had died for me, and I wanted to show my gratitude to God by trying to walk with him. But to what extent? I knew I should read my Bible a little bit. I knew I should pray now and then. I knew I should get somewhat involved in my church. But how far did I need to take all this?

About that time a mature Christian man who knew me well sensed my struggle. "Bill," he said, "I have a challenge for you. Why not put your whole life in God's hands? If at any point he shows himself to be untrustworthy, then you can bail."

I decided there was little to lose. I might as well go for it. So I said, "Okay, God, I am making a decision today. I am going to give your leadership a try. I am all yours." How grateful I am that he was willing to respond to my calculated approach to faith with the gifts of his love and his guidance.

 OPEN

- Do you think people are more trusting or less trusting than they were ten years ago? Why do you think so?

■ What is the difference between being trusting and being gullible?

STUDY

Read Proverbs 3:1-4.

¹My son, do not forget my teaching,
    but keep my commands in your heart,
²for they will prolong your life many years
    and bring you prosperity.

³Let love and faithfulness never leave you;
    bind them around your neck,
    write them on the tablet of your heart.
⁴Then you will win favor and a good name
    in the sight of God and man.

1. Why is it so easy to forget wise teaching (v. 1)?

2. What do you think it means to keep the commands "in your heart" and "on the tablet of your heart" (vv. 1, 3)?

3. If we hold God's wisdom in our hearts, how will our lives be different (vv. 2, 4)?

Read Proverbs 3:5-8.
[5]Trust in the LORD with all your heart
    and lean not on your own understanding;
[6]in all your ways acknowledge him,
    and he will make your paths straight.

[7]Do not be wise in your own eyes;
    fear the LORD and shun evil.
[8]This will bring health to your body
    and nourishment to your bones.

---

4. How do the metaphors here show the difference between relying on God and relying on ourselves?

---

5. If we trust fully in God, what is the promised harvest in our lives?

---

6. When have you found these promises true?

Read Proverbs 3:9-12.

[9]Honor the LORD with your wealth,
    with the firstfruits of all your crops;
[10]then your barns will be filled to overflowing,
    and your vats will brim over with new wine.

[11]My son, do not despise the LORD's discipline
    and do not resent his rebuke,
[12]because the LORD disciplines those he loves,
    as a father the son he delights in.

---

7. This passage follows immediately after Proverbs 3:5-8. What connection do you see between the two passages?

---

8. Why does honoring the Lord with our firstfruits (not the leftovers) particularly require trust in him?

---

9. What do you think it means to "despise" the Lord's discipline?

10. In order to willingly submit to God's discipline, what must we believe about him?

---

11. What external or internal pressures do you feel to rely on your own wisdom rather than on God's?

How can you stand up to those pressures and choose God's wisdom instead?

 COMMIT

■ In what situations do you tend to rely on your own understanding?

■ How will you plan to listen less to yourself and more to the Lord in those situations?

As much as you are able, place your life fully in God's hands. Specifically name those areas where trust is difficult, and surrender them to the Lord.

For further reading: *Chapter twelve of* Making Life Work.

GUIDELINES FOR LEADERS

Leading a Bible discussion can be an enjoyable and rewarding experience. But it can also be intimidating—especially if you've never done it before. If this is how you feel, you're in good company.

Remember when God asked Moses to lead the Israelites out of Egypt? Moses replied, "O Lord, please send someone else to do it" (Ex 4:13). But God gave Moses the help (human and divine) he needed to be a strong leader.

Leading a Bible discussion is not difficult if you follow certain guidelines. You don't need to be an expert on the Bible or a trained teacher. The suggestions listed below can help you to effectively fulfill your role as leader—and enjoy doing it.

PREPARING FOR THE STUDY

1. As you study the passage ahead of time, ask God to help you understand it and apply it in your own life. Unless this happens, you will not be prepared to lead others. Pray too for the various members of the group. Ask God to open your hearts to the message of his Word and motivate you to action.

2. Read the introduction to the entire guide to get an overview of the subject at hand and the issues that will be explored.

3. Be ready for the "Open" questions with a personal story or example. The group will be only as vulnerable and open as its leader.

4. Read the chapter of the companion book that is suggested under "Further Reading" at the end of each study.

5. As you begin preparing for each study, read and reread the assigned Bible passage to familiarize yourself with it. You may want to look up the passage in a Bible so that you can see its context.

6. This study guide is based on the New International Version of the Bible. That is what is reproduced in your guide. It will help you and the group if you use this translation as the basis for your study and discussion.

7. Carefully work through each question in the study. Spend time in meditation and reflection as you consider how to respond.

8. Write your thoughts and responses in the space provided in the study guide. This will help you to express your understanding of the passage clearly.

9. It might help you to have a Bible dictionary handy. Use it to look up any unfamiliar words, names or places.

10. Take the final (application) questions and the "Commit" portion of each study seriously. Consider what this means for your life, what changes you may need to make in your lifestyle and/or what actions you can take in your church or with people you know. Remember that the group will follow your lead in responding to the studies.

LEADING THE STUDY

1. Be sure everyone in your group has a study guide and Bible. Encourage the group to prepare beforehand for each discussion by

reading the introduction to the guide and by working through the questions in the study.

2. At the beginning of your first time together, explain that these studies are meant to be discussions, not lectures. Encourage the members of the group to participate. However, do not put pressure on those who may be hesitant to speak during the first few sessions.

3. Begin the study on time. Open with prayer, asking God to help the group understand and apply the passage.

4. Have a group member read the introductory paragraph at the beginning of the discussion. This will remind the group of the topic of the study.

5. Every study begins with a section called "Open." These "approach" questions are meant to be asked before the passage is read. They are important for several reasons.

First, there is always a stiffness that needs to be overcome before people will begin to talk openly. A good question will break the ice.

Second, most people will have lots of different things going on in their minds (dinner, an exam, an important meeting coming up, how to get the car fixed) that have nothing to do with the study. A creative question will get their attention and draw them into the discussion.

Third, approach questions can reveal where our thoughts or feelings need to be transformed by Scripture. That is why it is especially important not to read the passage before the approach question is asked. The passage will tend to color the honest reactions people would otherwise give, because they feel they are supposed to think the way the Bible does.

6. Have a group member read aloud the passage to be studied.

7. As you ask the questions, keep in mind that they are designed to be used just as they are written. You may simply read them aloud. Or you may prefer to express them in your own words.

   There may be times when it is appropriate to deviate from the study guide. For example, a question may already have been answered. If so, move on to the next question. Or someone may raise an important question not covered in the guide. Take time to discuss it, but try to keep the group from going off on tangents.

8. Avoid answering your own questions. Repeat or rephrase them if necessary until they are clearly understood. An eager group quickly becomes passive and silent if members think the leader will give all the *right* answers.

9. Don't be afraid of silence. People may need time to think about the question before formulating their answers.

10. Don't be content with just one answer. Ask, "What do the rest of you think?" or, "Anything else?" until several people have given answers to a question.

11. Acknowledge all contributions. Be affirming whenever possible. Never reject an answer. If it is clearly off-base, ask, "Which verse led you to that conclusion?" or, "What do the rest of you think?"

12. Don't expect every answer to be addressed to you, even though this will probably happen at first. As group members become more at ease, they will begin to truly interact with each other. This is one sign of healthy discussion.

13. Don't be afraid of controversy. It can be stimulating! If you don't resolve an issue completely, don't be frustrated. Move on and keep it in mind for later. A subsequent study may solve the problem.

14. Periodically summarize what the group has said about the passage. This helps to draw together the various ideas mentioned and gives continuity to the study. But don't preach.

15. Don't skip over the application questions at the end of each study. It's important that we each apply the message of the passage to ourselves in a specific way. Be willing to get things started by describing how you have been affected by the study.

Depending on the makeup of your group and the length of time you've been together, you may or may not want to discuss the "Commit" section. If not, allow the group to read it and reflect on it silently. Encourage members to make specific commitments and to write them in their study guide. Ask them the following week how they did with their commitments.

16. Conclude your time together with conversational prayer. Ask for God's help in following through on the commitments you've made.

17. End on time.

Many more suggestions and helps are found in The Big Book on Small Groups *by Jeffrey Arnold.*

Study One.   PURSUE WISDOM. Proverbs 2:1-15.

> **Purpose:** *To commit ourselves to pursue*
> *God's wisdom for everyday living.*

Question 1.

The picture in verses 1-4 is not of a passive person who expects wisdom to float down from on high. The beginning phrase "my son" suggests intimate personal advice. Anyone who reads these words and takes them seriously is expected to turn their ear, apply their heart, call out, cry aloud, look and search as for hidden treasure. If we want to be wise, we must actively apply ourselves to seek out wisdom.

Question 5.

Much of the book of Proverbs is written in parallels: an idea is expressed in one phrase, then repeated in a slightly different form. Verse 5 pairs understanding the fear of the Lord with finding the knowledge of God. We fear God not because he is a stranger but because we know him and stand in awe of who he is. Proverbs 1:7 tells us that "The fear of the LORD is the beginning of knowledge, but fools despise wisdom and discipline."

"There is a mystery in divine holiness which produces in man a sense of terror. . . . But this kind of dread is not merely negative. It accompanies the perception of God's glory and may generate an emotion of exultation and joy at the discovery of God's intense concern and love for man. . . . This kind of fear is the result not only of the knowledge that Yahweh is a holy God, but also of the apprehension of his saving grace" (Samuel Terrien, "Fear," in *Interpreter's Dictionary of the Bible,* ed. George Arthur Buttrick et al. [Nashville, Tenn.: Abingdon, 1962], 2:257-58).

Question 6.

For a follow-up question, ask: "What are some other things that God gives but that also require our effort?" Many gifts of God require human beings to get involved and work hard. Farmers labor for a crop that ultimately comes from God's hand. Children must be born and nurtured. Even the most talented musicians must take lessons and diligently practice.

Study Two.   DEVELOP DISCIPLINE. Proverbs 6:6-11, 20-24.

Purpose: To see discipline as positive and to strive to develop discipline.

Question 1.

"The ant is referred to only twice in scripture (Prov. 6:6; 30:25). In both cases reference is made to the wisdom, foresight, or industriousness exercised in summer by these creatures in storing up food for winter" (W. W. Frerichs, "Ant," in *Interpreter's Dictionary,* 1:140).

Question 3.

This question is particularly appropriate for the contemporary working world. Since technology enables us to work from anywhere at any time, we can wind up working non-stop and feel guilty if we take an extended break. The same principle applies to anyone who has responsibilities at home, at church or in the community. If we get caught up in work for work's sake, we may need to discipline ourselves *not* to work at certain times for the sake of our families and our own well-being. The point of verses 6-8 is that the ant works hard to provide for its needs. It never engages in busy-work but is focused on the vital task at hand (or rather at leg).

Question 4.

Group members may tend to answer in generalizations rather than from personal experience. If this happens, share an instance when you suffered some failure due to your own lack of discipline. Your openness will encourage the group to admit problems they have in this area.

Question 5.

A little rest easily leads to a lot more rest. While rest is vital, we must be watchful or inertia will take over.

Question 6.

Regular reading of Scripture, hearing teaching and preaching of the Word, Bible memorization, and placing written Scripture where we will see it at the right time will help us "bind" God's wisdom to our hearts. Most important is a willing attitude. If our hearts are not open to God's commandments, the other activities will be empty ritual.

Question 7.

Use the ideas listed here to draw out stories and illustrations of how wisdom has guided group members.

Commit.

You might pair off to discuss where you are struggling, what steps you want to take and how to pray for each other. Or, in a larger group discussion, focus on the application rather than the confession of sin, and pray for each other.

Study Three. SPEAK TRUTH.
Proverbs 11:1, 3; 12:19, 22; 14:25; 15:4.

Purpose: To resolve to live in honesty before God and others.

Question 1.

"Although David and Ezekiel (45:10-12) both pronounced certain basic standards, these tended to vary. The purchaser often carried his own weights in a wallet (Prov 16:11) so that he could check on the merchants. Both the law and the prophets take a strong line on just weights and measures. General standards in business dealings are a fair indication of the spiritual state of a nation" ("Weights and Measures," in *Eerdmans' Handbook to the Bible,* ed. David Alexander and Pat Alexander [Grand Rapids, Mich.: Eerdmans, 1973], p. 104).

Question 4.

In general, experience shows us that lies succeed only temporarily and the truth eventually comes out. This is the common course of events in dishonest business dealings, extramarital affairs and all types of slander.

As with most of the Proverbs, 12:19 states a general principle that usually prevails; it is not an absolute guarantee that the truth will always be known in our lifetime. We can be assured that a liar's victory is seldom permanent in this life and never permanent in eternity. Truth endures forever because the eternal God is true. "All your words are true; all your righteous laws are eternal" (Ps 119:160). Jesus, God incarnate, stated "I am the way and the truth and the life" (Jn 14:6).

Question 5.

God sees through all lies. He has the power to let the truth be known even when it seems impossible. If someone lies about us, we can take comfort in the assurance that the Lord knows everything and will eventually vindicate us. We can call on him to defend us against lies (Ps 41; 144:7-8).

Question 7.

In a capital case, a truthful witness can literally save the life of a falsely accused person (and conversely, a lying witness can literally cause an innocent person to die).

Question 8.

This proverb, like many, is a parallelism. The deceitful tongue is contrasted with the tongue that brings healing—by implication an honest tongue. We may be tempted to gloss over a bad situation through dishonesty or evasion of the truth, but lies will never bring genuine healing.

Question 9.

Besides the obvious example from the law courts (question 7), there are many more routine ways in which honest words can heal and save lives. When people know we are being straightforward with them, they can drop their defensiveness and have confidence to be straightforward in return. Families, churches and communities are far happier when things are done openly with no hidden motives. A suspicious society is not a happy or healthy society. Suspicion separates people while honesty unites us.

Not that honesty is always comfortable. God may call us to bring healing and life to someone by confronting that person about destructive habits. I am tremendously grateful for people who have boldly confronted me and told me difficult truths I needed to hear.

Study Four. HONOR FAMILY.
             Proverbs 15:17; 17:1, 6; 19:18; 21:9, 19; 23:22.
             Purpose: To behave with honor, respect and love toward family members.

Questions 3-4.

While these proverbs appear to pick on the wife, they obviously extend to both husbands and wives. A quarrelsome and ill-tempered husband is no more pleasing to God than a quarrelsome and ill-tempered wife.

Traditional homes of the Middle East had (and still have) flat roofs that are easily accessible. A wealthy couple made a small room on their rooftop for the prophet Elijah to stay when he came through the area (2 Kings 4:8-10). Since the location could be dangerous, the Law prescribed that a barrier should be built around the rooftop (Deut 22:8). It was from a rooftop that David saw Bathsheba and desired her (2 Sam 11:2)—a warning for anyone whose spouse feels like retreating to the rooftop to get some peace! A desert in biblical times would be even less hospitable than a rooftop. To be banished to the desert would be to live with chronic thirst, oppressive heat in the day and cold at night.

Question 7.

Discipline is meant to bring about positive change. If a young person is going the wrong way and is developing harmful patterns of life, loving discipline can bring about change, and change brings hope for a better future.

Question 8.

Hebrews 12:5-11 expands on the fruit of discipline in our lives. This passage includes a quote from Proverbs 3:11-12, which we will look at in study 6.

Question 9.

Note that this passage clearly applies to adult children and not only to young children.

Study Five. MANAGE ANGER.
Proverbs 12:18; 15:1; 16:32; 19:19; 22:24-25; 29:22.

Purpose: To develop self-control by letting God rule our spirits.

Question 1.

There is possibly no quicker way to demolish a relationship than to blow up at someone in unreasonable fury. A one-time explosion can be forgiven, but if the blowups are chronic, people will hesitate to get close. A volatile person gets a reputation of being too unstable to take on important responsibilities at work or in church. The hot-tempered person sacrifices a secure home life, since the family is always uneasy if not frightened around him. A person with a bad temper keeps everyone on edge, fearful of the next blowup. While those around them obviously pay a price, bad-tempered people pay heavily along with them.

Question 10.

I once interviewed a decorated hero of the Vietnam War. After answering my questions about his life-and-death struggles in the war, he told me about an even greater challenge he faced after returning from the war: rebuilding his badly broken marriage. He claimed that it required less courage to charge into an enemy encampment in Vietnam than it took to swallow his pride, enter marriage counseling, and face the truth about himself and his patterns of relating to his wife.

Study Six.　TRUST GOD.　Proverbs 3:1-12.

Purpose: *To increasingly surrender every aspect of life to God.*

Question 3.

Long life and prosperity are promised to the one who holds the commands to heart. As we have seen with many of the proverbs, this statement is a general principle rather than an absolute guarantee of wealth and a long physical life. What is certain is that the person who belongs to God through Christ shares his eternal life and will live with him forever in heaven. The spiritual prosperity of the godly person is far more valuable than any material wealth. "Ill-gotten treasures are of no value, but righteousness delivers from death" (Prov 10:2).

Question 7.

Following God's wisdom, honoring him with our material goods and accepting his discipline are all sure signs of trust in him. Without trust, we would resist his guidance and hold back our gifts. In addition, these proverbs all promise that trust in God will be rewarded.

Question 8.

When we give to the Lord first, rather than take care of our own needs first, we put ourselves in a position of depending on him to supply what we need. The principle of giving the firstfruits to the Lord was crucial to Old Testament law (for example, see Lev 22:9-14; Deut 26:1-15).

CHRISTIAN BASICS BIBLE STUDIES
FROM INTERVARSITY PRESS

Christian Basics are the keys to becoming a mature disciple. The studies in these guides, based on material from some well-loved books (which can be read along with the studies), will take you through key Scripture passages and help you to apply biblical truths to your life. Each guide has six studies for individuals or groups.

CERTAINTY: *Know Why You Believe* by Paul Little. Faith means facing hard questions. Is Jesus the only way to God? Why does God allow suffering and evil? These questions need solid answers. These studies will guide you to Scripture to find a reasonable response to the toughest challenges you face.

CHARACTER: *Who You Are When No One's Looking* by Bill Hybels. Courage. Discipline. Vision. Endurance. Compassion. Self-sacrifice. The qualities covered in this Bible study guide provide a foundation for character. With this foundation and God's guidance, we can maintain character even when we face temptations and troubles.

CHRIST: *Basic Christianity* by John Stott. God himself is seeking us through his Son, Jesus Christ. But who is this Jesus? These studies explore the person and character of the man who has altered the face of history. Discover him for the first time or in a new and deeper way.

COMMITMENT: *My Heart—Christ's Home* by Robert Boyd Munger. What would it be like to have Christ come into the home of our hearts? Moving from the living room to the study to the recreation room with him, we discover what he desires for us. These studies will take you through six rooms of your heart. You will be stretched and enriched by your personal meetings with Christ in each study.

DECISIONS: *Finding God's Will* by J. I. Packer. Facing a big decision? From job changes to marriage to buying a house, this guide will give you the biblical grounding you need to discover what God has in store for you.

EXCELLENCE: *Run with the Horses* by Eugene Peterson. Life is difficult. Daily we must choose whether to live cautiously or courageously. God calls us to live at our best, to pursue righteousness, to sustain a drive toward excellence. These studies on Jeremiah's pursuit of excellence with God's help will motivate and inspire you.

HOPE: *Never Beyond Hope* by J. I. Packer and Carolyn Nystrom. Ever feel like a hopeless sinner? Look at the lives of Samson, Peter, Martha and more. The Bible was given to us to offer hope and encouragement through the testimonies of those that have gone before us. Through this guide, you'll discover that just as biblical characters failed, biblical characters were redeemed. And God wants to do the same for you.

PERSEVERANCE: *A Long Obedience in the Same Direction* by Eugene Peterson. When the going gets tough, what does a Christian do? This world is no friend to grace. God has given us some resources, however. As we grow in character qualities like hope, patience, repentance and joy, we will grow in our ability to persevere. The biblical passages in these studies offer encouragement to continue in the path Christ has set forth for us.

PRAYER: *Too Busy Not to Pray* by Bill Hybels. There's so much going on— work, church, school, family, relationships: the list is never-ending. Someone always seems to need something from us. But time for God, time to pray, seems impossible to find. These studies are designed to help you slow down and listen to God so that you can respond to him.

PRIORITIES: *Tyranny of the Urgent* by Charles Hummel. Have you ever wished for a thirty-hour day? Every week we leave a trail of unfinished tasks. Unanswered letters, unvisited friends and unread books haunt our waking moments. We desperately need relief. This guide is designed to help you put your life back in order by discovering what is *really* important. Find out what God's priorities are for you.

TRANSFORMATION: *Developing a Heart for God* by Rebecca Manley Pippert. Would you like to move from despair to hope? Would you like to transform your feelings of fear to faith? Would you like to turn envy into compassion? The Bible shows us how David turned these negative emotions in his life into godly character qualities. By studying his life and choices we can make the same transformation in our own lives.

WISDOM: *Making Life Work* by Bill Hybels. Some people spend their lives relying on the abundance of information that's out there. But sometimes knowledge isn't enough. When we're stuck and don't know where to turn for answers, Proverbs offers practical advice and spiritual wisdom for real-life questions so that we might become people who think and act out of godly wisdom.

WITNESSING: *How to Give Away Your Faith* by Paul Little. If you want to talk about Jesus, but you're not sure what to say—or how to say it—this Bible study guide is for you. It will deepen your understanding of the essentials of faith and strengthen your confidence as you talk with others.